ENGLISH GRAMMAR

Robyn Gee and Carol Watson

Designed and illustrated by
Kim Blundell

Consultant: Diccon Swan

Contents

With thanks t... ...ol, Dorset.

D0529004

What is grammar?

Grammar is a set of rules and guidelines to help you use language correctly. If you want to learn a trade or skill you have to know how to handle the tools of the trade. If you want to express yourself well you have to know how to handle the tools of language.

Why should we have rules?

Rules always seem boring, dull and pointless, and breaking rules is fun. But imagine you were playing a game of cricket. Like all games it is based on a set of rules. If some of the players in the team decided to break the rules and do what they wanted, the game would become chaotic. You would not know what was happening and everyone would become confused.

This can also happen with language. If you do not follow the guidelines it will lose its meaning and people will not understand what you are trying to communicate.

How can grammar help?

Most of us ignore grammar in our everyday speech and in writing quick messages. It is, however, important to be accurate, clear and formal in certain aspects of life:

1. Jobs

Nowadays it is difficult to find a job. No matter how talented or well-qualified you are at something, there always seem to be hundreds of other people just as suitable.

If you apply for a job sending a letter which is full of grammatical mistakes, the employer will give preference to someone with the same qualifications who has expressed himself correctly.

2. Other kinds of letters and communications

Sometimes you may want to write or speak to someone in authority. It could be to explain a situation, complain about something or even to make someone see your point of view.

It's like this officer...

If you can express yourself clearly and concisely the point you are making will be easily understood. If, however, you write or speak in a rambling, unintelligible way which does not convey your point of view, people may take advantage of you or misinterpret what you say.

3. Creative writing

There are times when you may want to write something creative, like a poem, a story, or even just your thoughts. Many people feel that in this case it is not important to write correctly as it prevents you from writing spontaneously. This can be true. If, however, you want to add style and variety to this kind of expression, and to convey it effectively to others, it will help if you have some knowledge of how the English language works.

What shall I write today?

Most famous writers, artists and musicians have based their creative talents on some kind of rules.

Parts of speech

What we say is called speech. Speech is rather like a train. It can be in one long burst, or it can be lots of short ones (little trains going in different directions).

Like a train it is made up of carriages or trucks which by themselves do not do very much, but, when linked together to form the train, they are very useful.

The trucks are like the words in speech — they can be individual things but they need others to make them into a useful whole.

The whole train is like a sentence — a group of words that makes sense and gets us somewhere. Trains also have to keep on the lines in order to get anywhere, and the track is like grammar; it lays down the direction and makes sure the train gets somewhere.

In this book you will find all the different parts of speech you can use, and how to join them into different kinds of sentences. You will also find tips on how to avoid common mistakes in English, and hints on how to write English clearly and with style.

As you read you may well come across words you have never met before. If so, try looking in the index/glossary where there is an explanation of some of the harder words.

Grammar will keep you on the right lines.

The parts of speech — brief guide

There are eight different parts of speech:

1. Noun

Word used for naming a person, animal, place or thing (e.g. William, mouse, shop, ladder).

2. Pronoun

Word used to refer to a person or thing without giving a name. Takes the place of a noun (e.g. he, she, them, him).

4. Adjective

Word used to describe a *noun* or *pronoun* (e.g. fat, dangerous, new, wooden).

4. Verb

Often called a "doing" word. Word used to describe action or existence (e.g. run, was, kicked, are).

5. Adverb

Word used generally to modify (tell you more about) a *verb*, but can tell you more about any word other than a noun or pronoun (e.g. quickly, soon, very, rather).

6. Preposition

Word used for showing what one person or thing has to do with another person or thing — usually where they are in relation to one another (e.g. with, under, on).

7. Conjunction

Word used to join words and clauses (e.g. and, but, when).

8. Interjection (or Exclamation)

Word used to express exclamation (e.g. Oh! Hello).

3

Nouns

A noun is a word used for naming a person, an animal, a place or a thing.

These words are all nouns.

| bird | ladder | windowcleaner | shop |

To decide whether a word is a noun, ask yourself, "Does it tell me something's name?" If the answer is, "Yes", the word is a noun.

under ✗

table ✓

Does it tell me the name of something?

Nouns can usually have "the", or "a", or "an" in front of them. Try putting "the" in front of the words on the right to find out which of them are nouns.

saucepan	heat
finger	daffodil
happy	never
rocket	sky
sometime	have

Can I say "the never"?

Names of particular people are nouns, even though you can't put "the" in front of them.

Alice   **Albert**   **Ethel**

Spot the nouns

Can you pick out the nouns in the list of words below?

ugly	under
box	slowly
David	in
wonderful	cup
dog	when
bottle	silly

How many nouns can you find in the sentences below?

1. Boris, the cat, ran across the road.
2. Cynthia was wearing a beautiful red dress.
3. Tom had a dog, a hamster, a white rabbit and a budgerigar.
4. Mary has sold her old car in favour of a new bicycle.
5. The poor old man had only a bed, a table and one chair.

Singular or plural

Nouns can be either singular (referring to one single person or thing):

| bat | box | berry |

Is this singular or plural?

It is singular.

or plural:

| bats | boxes | berries |

leaf

4

Four kinds of nouns

There are four different kinds of nouns.
These are: 1. *proper* nouns, 2. *common* nouns, 3. *collective* nouns, 4. *abstract* nouns.

1. *A proper noun* is a noun that refers to a particular person or thing, rather than a general class of thing.

Samson
Mexico
Monday
August
Gulliver's Travels

Proper nouns have capital letters.

You can't usually put "the" or "a" with proper nouns.

2. *A common noun* names a kind of person or thing. It is called "common" because the name is common to all persons or things of the same kind.

man
country
day
month
book

Compare these words with the proper nouns shown above.

3. *A collective noun* describes a group or collection of people or things.

These words are all collective nouns.

army (a collection of soldiers)
bunch (a collection of flowers)
team (a collection of players)
pack (a collection of hounds)
swarm (a collection of bees)

Some collective nouns describe a definite number of something. "Pair" and "dozen" are both collective nouns.

4. *Abstract nouns* describe things that cannot actually be seen, heard, smelt, felt or tasted.

sleep
honesty
boredom
freedom
power

Gender A noun is either masculine, feminine, common or neuter in gender.

actor   actress   teacher   book

Common (either masculine or feminine)

Neuter (neither masculine nor feminine)

Masculine   Feminine

Pronouns

Sometimes you refer to a person or thing not by its actual name, but by another word which stands for it. The word you use to stand for a noun is called a pronoun (which means "for a noun").

Jack plays his oboe every evening. He is learning very fast.

"He" is a pronoun. In this sentence it stands for Jack.

To decide if a word is a pronoun ask yourself, "Does it stand for a noun?"

You use pronouns so that you do not have to repeat the same nouns over again. They make speaking and writing much quicker and clearer. Compare the two sentences below.

When Barnaby stroked the cat and listened to it purring softly, he felt calm and peaceful.

Pronoun

If there were no pronouns you would have to say this.

When Barnaby stroked the cat and listened to the cat purring softly, Barnaby felt calm and peaceful.

The words in the boxes below are all pronouns. They can all stand instead of the name of a person, place or thing.

The words in the pink column are singular and stand for singular nouns.

The words in the blue column are plural and stand in the place of plural nouns.

"I" is the only pronoun that is always spelt with a capital letter.

The words along the top are used when the pronoun is the subject[1] of a sentence.

The words in the middle are used when the pronoun is an object[2] in a sentence.

The words along the bottom are used to show that something belongs to someone.

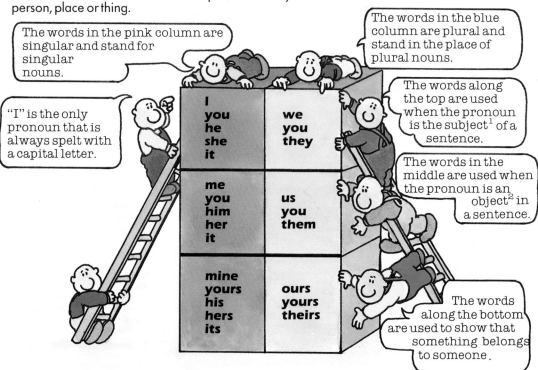

I you he she it	we you they
me you him her it	us you them
mine yours his hers its	ours yours theirs

[1] & [2]. To find out about subjects and objects in a sentence see page 10.

Problems with "I" and "me"

In some sentences it is difficult to decide whether to use "me" or "I".

Would you say this?

Or this?

Carol and me are going on holiday.

Carol and I are going on holiday.

Whenever you find it difficult to decide, try splitting the sentence into two short sentences, like this:

Carol is going on holiday.

You could not say this, could you?

I am going on holiday.

Me am going on holiday.

✓ Carol and I are going on holiday.

This sentence was the correct one.

After prepositions* you always use the object form of the pronoun.

Would you say this?

It is a secret between Jo and I.

or this?

It is a secret between Jo and me.

"between" is a preposition.

This one is right.

Find the pronouns

Can you find the pronouns in these sentences?

1. She went out to find them.
2. We asked him if he was feeling better.
3. "I think this is yours," she said.
4. You should ask her if she wants to join us.
5. It isn't yours, it's mine!
6. They took me home with them.

Other types of pronoun

The pronouns shown in the chart on the opposite page are called personal pronouns and are probably used more than any others. But there are several other types of pronoun. Here is a list of some of the different types:

1. **Personal pronouns** (I, you, etc.).

2. **Reflexive pronouns** (myself, yourself, himself, herself, itself, ourselves, themselves). These are called reflexive because they *reflect* back to an earlier noun or pronoun.

3. **Relative pronouns** (who, whom, whose, which, that, what). These pronouns help to connect or *relate* one part of a sentence to another.

4. **Interrogative pronouns** (who, whose, whom, which, what). These pronouns help to ask questions or *interrogate*.

5. **Demonstrative pronouns** (this, that, these, those). These point out a person or thing specifically.

6. **Indefinite pronouns** (words like any, each, several, some, and many more). These refer to people or things generally rather than specifically.

7

*See pages 18 and 19.

Adjectives

An adjective is a word which "qualifies" (tells you more about) a noun or pronoun. It answers the question, "What is it like?".

This tells you about the jacket.

The burglar was wearing a *black* jacket, a *furry* hat and a *large* mask over his face.

This tells you more about the hat.

This word tells you more about the mask.

An adjective usually comes before a noun but sometimes it can be separated from its noun and come afterwards.

Ben looked *frightened*.

The traffic warden in our area is very *fierce*.

Different types of adjectives

1. *"Asking" adjectives (interrogative)*

Which hat do you prefer?

"What" is another asking adjective.

2. *Possessive adjectives* — these show ownership.

Sue never brushes *her* hair.

This shows you *whose* hair it is.

Other possessive adjectives are:

my	our	their	his	your

3. *Adjectives of number or quantity* — these deal with the *amount* of something.

All numbers are adjectives.

She invited *five* friends for breakfast.

She did not have *any* food left.

Here are some adjectives of quantity:

much more most little less least no some any enough sufficient all whole half quarter

4. *"Pointing-out" adjectives (demonstrative)*

These are singular.

That man stole *this* handbag.

Those apples and these pears are bad.

These are plural.

Comparing things

1. There are three forms of any adjective that you can use when you describe a noun or pronoun. Look at the sentences below:

She is tall.

The word *tall* is an ordinary adjective.

> You use a comparative adjective when you are *comparing* two people or things.

She is taller than her sister.

The word *taller* is a *comparative* adjective.

She is the tallest in her family.

The word *tallest* is a *superlative* adjective.

> You use a superlative when referring to at least three people or things.

The comparative adjective is made by adding -er to the adjective, and the superlative is made by adding -est to the adjective and putting *the* in front of it.

2. Some adjectives have to change their spelling slightly to form their comparatives and superlatives.

a. If the adjective ends in an "e", you just add -r for the comparative and -st for the superlative.

large   larger   largest

b. If the adjective ends in "y", this letter is changed to "i" before adding -er and -est.

pretty   prettier   prettiest

> "y" changes to "i".

c. Some adjectives double their final letter before adding -er and -est.

thin   thinner   thinnest

3. Where adding -er and est would make an adjective sound awkward, you form the comparative and superlative by putting *more* and *the most* in front of it.

She is beautiful.

She is more beautiful.

She is the most beautiful.

> Longer words often sound awkward if you add -er or -est to them.

4. Some of the most common adjectives form their comparatives and superlatives in an odd or "irregular" way that does not follow the normal rules.

Adjective	Comparative	Superlative
good	better	best
bad	worse	worst
little	less	least
much	more	most
many	more	most

Verbs

A verb is a word, or a group of words, that tells you what a person or thing is being or doing. It is often called a *doing word*: e.g. running, eating, sitting.

A verb is the most important word in a sentence; without it a sentence does not make any sense.

He *drank* his tea.	He his tea.
She *went* to the shops.	She to the shops.

These don't make sense at all.

All sentences have a *subject* and a *verb*. The subject is the person or thing doing the action.

Cats purr.

The wind blows.

Birds fly.

Some sentences can be just the subject and the verb, but in some sentences the verb has to have an *object* as well.

Cats chase *mice.*

Alice liked *Ben.*

King Alfred burnt *the cakes.*

The object tells you "what" or "whom" the verb affects.

King Alfred burnt what? King Alfred burnt *the cakes.*

Think of all the actions you can do. These are all verbs.

Transitive and intransitive verbs

When a verb takes the action from the subject across to the object it is called a *transitive* verb.

Squirrels collect nuts.

Here the squirrel is doing the action to the nuts.

Tom polished his shoes.

The verbs that don't have any objects are called *intransitive* verbs.

Your socks smell.

The boat sank.

The telephone rang.

Intransitive verbs make sense on their own; they do not need an object.

Some verbs can be both transitive and intransitive.

He smells. He smelt the burning toast.	She is playing. She is playing the piano.

The infinitive

The infinitive is *the name* of the verb, e.g. go, catch, run, sleep. It usually has "to" in front of it, but you can use it without.

to wish

> **She began *to wish* she had never set out.**

to go

> **Bill did not know where *to go*.**

(to) work

> **Our teacher makes us *work* hard.**

This would sound odd with "to" in front of it.

Tenses

The word "tense" comes from the Latin word "tempus" — meaning time. The tense of the verb tells you the time at which the action takes place.

There are three main tenses:

Present

I eat.

Past

I ate.

Future

I shall eat.

Look at the chart below. It will help you sort out how the verbs and tenses work. The verb "to stay" is used as an example.

Subject	Present	Past	Future
I	stay (am staying)	stayed (was staying)	shall stay (shall be staying)
you (singular)	stay (are staying)	stayed (were staying)	will stay (will be staying)
he/she/it	stays (is staying)	stayed (was staying)	will stay (will be staying)
we	stay (are staying)	stayed (were staying)	shall stay (shall be staying)
you (plural)	stay (are staying)	stayed (were staying)	will stay (will be staying)
they	stay (are staying)	stayed (were staying)	will stay (will be staying)

The verbs in brackets are another version of the verb above them. This is called the *continuous* tense because it shows that the action is going on for some time.

11

Auxiliary (helping) verbs

to be   to have

A verb is often made up of more than one word:

| He is talking. | They have worked. | We shall be running. |

The actual verb-word is helped out by parts of the special verbs: the verb *to be* and the verb *to have*. These helping verbs are called *auxiliary* verbs. They help to form the tenses.

| I *was* eating. | I *have* slept. |

shall   will

1 *Shall* and *will* are also parts of verbs. They help to make the future tense. *Shall* is used with *I* and *we*; all the other pronouns * use *will*.

| I *shall* return. | You *will* be late. |

2 You can use *shall* and *will* to show a command, a promise or an expression of determination. In order to do this you change the rule around.

instead of: | I shall go out. |

you use: | I *will* go out. |

instead of: | He will get up soon. |

You do this to stress the point you are making.

you use: | He *shall* get up soon. |

Spot the verb

Can you spot the verbs below?:

1. Diana cleaned the floor.

2. The dog is barking.

3. Dad has made the tea.

4. Jo will be watching the match.

5. Mum has crashed the car.

6. The chef is tossing a pancake.

Fill in the missing verb

Can you fill in the missing verb?

1. We . . . . going on holiday soon.
2. The baby . . . . been crying all day.
3. They . . . . be late if they don't hurry.
4. I . . . . miss you when you go.
5. I . . . . *not* do as you say!
6. Tom . . . . mending the fuse.
7. They . . . . working for hours.

12

* For more about pronouns see pages 6 and 7.

Active and passive

You can use verbs in two different ways.
These are often called "voices".

1. The active "voice"

Look at this sentence.

> **Tom *kicked* the ball.**

Here Tom (subject) is doing the action of kicking. *Kicked* is an *active* verb.

2. The passive "voice"

You can say the above sentence the other way round.

> **The ball *was kicked* by Tom.**

Here the ball (subject) is having the action done to it. *Was kicked* is a *passive* verb.

The active "voice" is stronger and more direct than the passive "voice". The active is used much more often because it is usually shorter and easier to read.

These are much easier.

Active	Passive
James *caught* ten fish.	**Ten fish *were caught* by James.**
Mum *baked* five cakes.	**Five cakes *were baked* by Mum.**

If you use the passive voice it can give a different kind of emphasis to your sentences. For example, when you see public notices they are often written in the passive because it is less aggressive and abrupt than the active.

These are less hostile.

Smoking is not allowed.	not	**We do not allow smoking!**
Dogs must be kept on a lead.	not	**Keep your dog on a lead!**

Change around

Can you change these sentences so that the verbs are in the *passive* voice?

1. The cat ate a huge, black spider.
2. Doris cleans the silver every fortnight.
3. Mum mowed the lawn early this morning.
4. The burglars hid the money under the bed.
5. Jo threw the rubbish into the dustbin.
6. The groom brushed the horse.
7. The gardener waters the plants.
8. He ordered a taxi to take her home.

Participles

Participles are parts of a verb. They are called participles because they "participate", or take part, in forming the verb. They usually follow the auxiliary verbs "to be" and "to have".[1]

Participles help to form the tenses of verbs, but they can also act as other parts of speech as well. There are two kinds of participle: past and present.

Past participle

The past participle helps to make the past tense of a verb. It usually follows "has", "have", "had" or "was".

The past participle usually ends in *-ed, -d, -t, -en* or *-n*.

Kim was *bitten* by a mosquito.

Tom had *fallen* out of bed.

Harriet has *walked* home.

heard
learnt
chosen
moved

dug
bought
begun
gone

But here are some examples of irregular endings.

The past participle as an adjective

The past participle can be used as an adjective as well as a verb.

These are verbs.

Jane wore a *creased* dress.

Jane's dress was *creased.*

Jim could not write with his *broken* pencil.

Jim's pencil had *broken.*

These are adjectives.

Can you see which nouns the adjectives are describing?

Present participle

The present participle is the part of the verb which ends in *-ing*.

The baby is *crying.*

Although it is called the *present* participle it is used to form *all* tenses with the help of the auxiliary verbs, "to have" and "to be".

Doris has been *cleaning* the house all day.

Graham is *working.*

We will be *going* tomorrow.

Verbs using the present participle are said to be in the continuous tense[2] whether past, present or future.

14

[1]See page 12.   [2]See page 11.

The present participle as an adjective

In the sentences below the present participle is used as an adjective.

> She painted a picture of the *rising* sun.

> She could not sleep for the noise of *chirping* birds, *braying* donkeys, *howling* dogs and *whining* mosquitoes.

Can you think of any more participles that can be used in this way?

Beware

It is very easy to get confused when using the present participle as an adjective or in adjectival phrases. People often use it wrongly.

Look at this sentence:

✗
> Driving along the road, a cow appeared in front of me.

This means a cow was driving along the road.

When the participle is acting as an adjective it qualifies a noun or pronoun like any other adjective. In the sentence above the adjectival participle is qualifying "cow" which creates the wrong impression.

If you are not sure whether you have used a participle correctly, try to re-phrase the sentence to avoid the problem.

> As I was driving along the road, a cow appeared in front of me. ✓

The present participle as a noun (gerund)

The present participle can be used as a noun. When it is used in this way it is called a *gerund*.

> Edward did not approve of the *hunting* of animals and the *shooting* of birds.

> The *giggling* of the girls annoyed the boys.

Notice that you can put "the" in front of it like any other noun.

A gerund acts just like any other noun, therefore it can be described by an adjective.

> The *awful wailing* of tom-cats went on all night.

> The *vicious killing* of the old man shocked everyone.

Beware

You always use a possessive *adjective* instead of a pronoun with a gerund.

> People regretted *his* going. ✓
> not People regretted him going. ✗

Remember.

> I don't like *your* being here. ✓
> not I don't like you being here. ✗

15

Adverbs

An adverb modifies (makes more precise) any word in a sentence other than a noun or a pronoun. Usually it tells you more about the verb.

An adverb nearly always answers the questions How? When? Where? or Why?

Look at this sentence:

> **Ben returned.**

It makes complete sense on its own, but you don't know how, when, where or why Ben returned. You can say more about Ben's return by using adverbs, or adverbial phrases.[1]

> **Ben returned _home_ (where) _quickly_ (how), _yesterday_ (when), _to watch the match_ (why).**

Adverbs can be one word or a group of words. When there is a group of words not containing a verb, it is a _phrase._ If the group of words contains a verb but does not make complete sense on its own, it is a _clause._[2]

Adverbs of degree

All the adverbs above modify the verb "returned". But adverbs can also modify adjectives and other adverbs. These are sometimes called _adverbs of degree_. All adverbs of degree answer the question _How?_

> Here the adverb tells you more about the adjective.

> **It was _too_ hot to play tennis.**

> **Mum looked _very_ different with her new hairstyle.**

> **Tom got up _remarkably_ early this morning.**

> **He painted the garden wall _rather_ carelessly.**

> Here the adverb modifies _another_ adverb.

Forming adverbs

Most adverbs in English end in -ly and come from adjectives.

soft	– softly
right	– rightly

Note! If the adjective ends in -y, e.g. pretty, you change the "y" into "i" before adding the -ly.

busy	– busily
weary	– wearily

Beware

Don't confuse adverbs with _adjectives_ that end in -ly.

> **prickly, manly, friendly**

> These are adjectives.

If you want to make an adverb out of adjectives like these, you turn them into adverbial phrases.

> **He chatted friendlily.** ✗

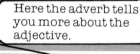

> You can't do this.

> **He chatted _in a friendly way_.** ✓

[1]See page 24.   [2]See page 25.

Sentence adverbs

Adverbs can appear in a sentence on their own. They can change the whole meaning of that sentence. These are called *sentence adverbs*.

Here are some sentence adverbs.

nevertheless   still   moreover

however   on the other hand

> She felt, *however,* that he was not entirely honest.

> He was, *nevertheless,* a loyal friend.

Placing the adverb

Make sure that you place adverbs in the sentence correctly, otherwise the meaning of the sentence may change or become confused.
    These *common adverbs* are often put in the wrong place.

only   just   almost   even   mainly   also

These should be placed immediately *before* the word they modify.

Look at this sentence:

> Pat gave Polly a pound.

ONLY

Try inserting "only" in every possible position in the sentence. How many different meanings can you make?

Adverb or adjective?

Some words can be either adverbs or adjectives depending on what they do in a sentence, e.g. fast, hard, late.

If they answer the questions How? When? Where? or Why? they are adverbs: but if they answer the question "What is it like?" they are adjectives, and will be telling you more about a specific noun.

> LIfe is *hard.* (adjective)

> Kim works *hard.* (adverb)

> The train arrived *early.* (adverb)

> I took an *early* train. (adjective)

Can you think of any more adverbs that can be used as adjectives?

Worn-out adverbs

Nowadays people tend to use certain adverbs of degree to stress what they are saying, when in fact they add little or nothing at all to the meaning of the sentence.

This letter will give you an idea of what to avoid.

Dear Sarah,
Thank you <u>awfully</u> for your note.
    I had an <u>absolutely</u> fabulous holiday, got <u>terribly</u> brown and met some <u>incredibly</u> interesting people.
We went to some <u>frightfully</u> expensive restaurants and had some <u>superbly</u> delicious meals!
We must meet soon,
    love Claude.

The adverbs underlined do not add much to the meaning of the sentence and lessen the effect of the adjectives.

17

Prepositions

Prepositions are words which show the relationship of one thing to another. They often tell you *where* one thing is in relation to another, or the "position" that it is in. They are always attached to a noun or pronoun.

| **The boots are *on* the table.** |

Where are the boots? — *On* the table.

| **Fred goes running *before* breakfast.** |

On is a preposition which shows the relationship between "the table" and "the boots".

Here are some more examples of prepositions:

| ***across* the road** | ***over* the fence** | ***into* the garden** | ***past* the dustbins** |

| ***under* a tree** | ***up* the stairs** | ***in* the bath** | ***down* the bannisters** |

Preposition or adverb?

Words that are prepositions can also do the work of adverbs. It is often difficult to sort out which is which. The best way to decide is to remember that a preposition is *always* followed by a noun or a pronoun.

| **The cat climbed *up* the tree.** |

Up is a *preposition* which tells you the relationship between "the cat" and "the tree".

| **The cat climbed *up*.** |

Up is an *adverb* which tells you *where* the cat climbed.

Here are some of the prepositions which can be used as adverbs:

| in | on | before | behind | near |
| below | along | through | down | over | under |

Prepositions and pronouns

If a preposition is followed by a pronoun the pronoun is always in its *object form.*[1]

✓	**She sat near *me*.**

	She sat near *I*.	✗

✓	**He gave it to *her*.**

	He gave it to *she*.	✗

Sometimes a preposition is followed by two words linked by *and*.

Look at these sentences:

> **A strange thing happened to *me*.**

> **A strange thing happened to *David* and *me*.**

> **A strange thing happened to David and *I*.** ✗

If you changed the noun David to a pronoun, *both* pronouns would be in the object form.

> **A strange thing happened to *him* and *me*.**

Who and whom?

The pronoun[2] *who* changes to *whom* after a preposition.

> **They are the people *to whom* I spoke.**

> **He is someone *for whom* I have great respect.**

Prepositions often confused

in/into

In is used to indicate a position.

> **The children are *in* bed.**

> **He is *in* the swimming pool.**

Into is used with a verb of motion to show entrance.

> **The children climbed *into* bed.**

> **He fell *into* the swimming pool.**

to/till/until

a. The word *to* can be used for place *and* time; *till* and *until* can be used for time only.

> *or*   **We work from 8.00 a.m. *to* 6.00 p.m.**
> **We work from 8.00 a.m. *till* 6.00 p.m.**

If there is no *from*, you use *till* or *until* instead of *to*.

> **We worked *until* dawn.**

b. The word *to* is used for place.

> **He drove *to* the crossroads.**

You can't write: ✗

> **He drove *until* the crossroads.**

[1]See pages 6-7.   [2]See page 7.

Connecting words (Conjunctions)

Words used to connect other words are called conjunctions. They join together words, phrases, clauses and sentences. Below you can see four conjunctions, each joining two words together.

> Conjunctions are connecting words.

Bill *and* Ben

| sad *but* true |

| young *yet* wise |

| friends *or* enemies |

Conjunctions are important for linking sentences together. Without them speech and writing would sound very jerky.

Look at these sentences:

| Jim turned round. | | Jim bumped into the fat lady. |

| Jim turned round *and* bumped into the fat lady. |

> Jim is the subject of both sentences so you can leave out the second Jim when you join the two sentences together

Conjunction pairs

Conjunctions often appear in pairs.

| He likes *both* jam *and* honey. |

| Cedric owns *not only* a house *but also* a castle. |

| Joanne is *neither* good *nor* clever. |

| They cannot decide *whether* to stay *or* go. |

Beware   When you use these pairs of conjunctions you have to make sure you put the conjunctions *before* the words they join.

| Rod *not only* played the guitar *but also* the drums. |

| Rod played *not only* the guitar *but also* the drums. |

| She *neither* was at home *nor* at work. | | She was *neither* at home *nor* at work. |

Different kinds of conjunctions

1. Certain conjunctions are used to join two sentences of equal importance. These are called *co-ordinating* conjunctions.

| and but for or yet however |
| as well as so nor both therefore |

| **Simon likes coffee.** | **Anna likes tea.** |

These two sentences are just as important as each other.

Simon likes coffee, *but* **Anna likes tea.**

| **She went to the shops.** | **She bought a box of chocolates.** |

She went to the shop *and* **bought a box of chocolates.**

2. Sometimes you join two sentences together so that one of them contains a major statement (main clause)★, and the other contains a minor statement (the subordinate clause)★. The conjunctions used to do this are called *subordinating* conjunctions.

These are the main statements.

He was angry *because* **I was late.**

| like before if while until |
| though because |
| although unless since |
| as where |
| whenever wherever |

Emma cleaned her teeth *before* **she went to bed.**

3. When you want to join two contrasting statements you can use particular conjunctions which add weight to the point you are making.

| though although however but |
| nevertheless |

Kim was very tired, *nevertheless* **she worked all weekend.**

She did not stop to rest *although* **she felt ill.**

What is missing?

Can you fill in the missing conjunctions in the sentences below?

1. Henry got up late . . . . he was on holiday.
2. He wanted to have a bath . . . . the water was cold.
3. He did not know . . . . to wear his jeans . . . . his shorts.
4. He ate a plateful of bacon . . . . eggs, ... drinking five cups of tea.

Which pair?

Can you put the correct pair of conjunctions into these sentences?

1. Celia could not decide . . . . it was true . . . . not.
2. They owned . . . . . a Mercedes . . . . a Range Rover.
3. This child is . . . . laughing . . . . crying.
4. Alice is . . . . tall . . . . short; she is average height.
5. Sam has . . . . a car . . . . a motorbike.

★See page 25.

Sentences

A sentence is a group of words which makes complete sense on its own.

A sentence has two parts – the person or thing which the sentence is about, called *the subject*; and what is written or said about the subject, called *the predicate*.

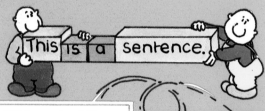

This is a sentence.

Look at this sentence:

James fell off his motorbike.

James is the subject of the sentence; the rest of the sentence is the predicate.

The predicate always includes the verb of the sentence.

fell off his motorbike.

This is the verb.

Sometimes the subject can be a group of words:

James, tired and weary from so much work, fell off his motorbike.

Who fell? "James, tired and weary from so much work," fell and is the *subject*.

The subject of the sentence is not always found at the beginning, it can also be in the middle or at the end. If it were always in the same place what we say and write would sound very boring.

The aeroplane flew over the mountains.

Over the mountains *the aeroplane* flew.

Over the mountains flew *the aeroplane*.

Sentences with a purpose

The sentences above are straightforward statements, but sentences can have different purposes:

1. **Statements** – sentences which state facts.

   It is very hot.

2. **Questions** – sentences which ask for an answer.

   Are you hot?

3. **Commands** – sentences which give orders or requests. (The subject of these sentences is usually understood and therefore not mentioned.)

   "(You) do not go out into the sun!"

4. **Exclamations** – sentences which express a strong feeling of emotion.

   My goodness, it's hot!

5. Greetings and sentences which don't have any definite form.

   Good morning. Many happy returns.

Simple sentences

A simple sentence has only *one* subject and *one* predicate.

> **The chef (subject) made a cake (predicate).**

It could take the form of a question:

> **Did the chef make a cake?**

or a command:

> **Make a cake!**

You can add any amount of adjectives[1] to the nouns:

> **The *jolly, fat* chef made an *enormous chocolate* cake.**

or any amount of adverbs[2] or adverbial phrases:[3]

> **The chef *happily* made a cake *in the kitchen after midnight.* (N.B. How? Where? When?)**

or both:

> **The jolly, fat chef happily made an enormous chocolate cake in the kitchen after midnight.**

Despite all the added description the sentence still has only *one subject* and *one verb*. It is still a simple sentence.

Compound sentences

If you used *simple* sentences all the time your writing and speech would sound very jerky. It is important to join sentences together to add variety to your language and make it flow.

A *compound* sentence is made up of two or more simple sentences joined by a conjunction[4] or separated by a comma, semi-colon or colon.

Here are two simple sentences.

> **The ship hit the rocks.**

> **It sank to the bottom of the sea.**

If you join them together with the conjunction "and" you can make a compound sentence.

> **The ship hit the rocks and it sank to the bottom of the sea.**

or,
> **Jane likes swimming.**

> **Fred likes to play tennis.**

> **Tom does not like to do anything at all.**

Join them with commas and a conjunction:

> **Jane likes swimming, Fred likes to play tennis, but Tom does not like to do anything at all.**

Note that the separate parts of the compound sentence still make complete sense if you take away the conjunction or punctuation.

23

[1]See pages 8 and 9.   [2]See page 16.   [3]See page 24.   [4]See pages 20 and 21.

Phrases

A phrase is a group of words which does not make complete sense on its own and *does not* contain a verb. It is not a complete sentence.

up the mountain

This does not make complete sense.

If you add a subject and a verb to this phrase you can make a complete sentence.

The climber (subject)   **struggled (verb)**

The climber struggled up the mountain.

If you want to write longer and more interesting sentences you can use phrases instead of adjectives, nouns and adverbs.

Adjectival phrases

In these sentences the phrases are used instead of adjectives.

> **The man *with the bow-tie* danced with the lady *in the red dress*.**

> **Matilda, *refreshed by a long holiday in Greece*, felt she could dance all night.**

Can you see which nouns they are describing?

Adverbial phrases

In the sentences below the phrases act as adverbs answering the question *How? When?* and *Where?* about the verb.

The bull charged angrily *across the field*.

Can you see which phrases answer the question how?

They climbed over a gate *as soon as possible* and ran *like the wind*.

Noun phrases

These phrases are acting as nouns in the sentences. They can do *all* the things that nouns can do.

Here they are the subject of the sentences.

All the people in the audience began to clap at the brilliant speech.

The terrier with short ears was well-trained by his master.

24

Clauses

A clause is a group of words which *does* contain a verb. It is part of a sentence.

MAIN

SUBORDINATE

when she went shopping

This does not make sense.

If, however, you add another clause to the one above, it does make sense in the sentence.

This is another clause

Sue bought a new dress when she went shopping.

Above there are two kinds of clauses: 1. *Main clause.* 2. *Subordinate clause.*

They are divided into two kinds according to the job they do in a sentence.

The most important clause is the *main clause.* This can stand by itself and make complete sense. It could be a sentence.

Richard ate five cream cakes

A *subordinate* clause is dependent on the main clause for its meaning.

because he was hungry

Clauses, like phrases, can do the work of adjectives, nouns and adverbs in a sentence. They make what you write more detailed and interesting.

Adjectival clause

These often begin with *who, which, that* or *whom.*

These are the nouns the clauses are describing

The boy *who had the longest legs* won the race.

David was a person *whom everyone respected.*

Adverbial clause

An adverbial clause does the work of an adverb (i.e. it answers the questions How? When? Where? or Why?).

How?

He ran *as fast as he could.*

When?

They sang *as they walked along.*

Where?

Robbers break in *where they see valuables kept.*

Can you see which verbs the clauses are describing?

Why?

I missed the train *because I was late.*

Noun clause

A noun clause can take the place of a noun. It can be the *subject* or *object* of the verb.

Here it is the subject.

That there is life after death is impossible to prove.

I want to know *what you have been doing* all day.

Here it is the object.

25

Complex sentences

A complex sentence is made up of a main clause[1] with one or more subordinate clauses.[2] Each clause always contains a verb.

The subordinate clauses can be noun, adjectival or adverbial clauses, and each one follows a preposition[3] or a conjunction.[4]

Look at the sentence below. The words in italics are verbs.

> **The man *limped* because his leg *hurt*.**

> **The man *limped* (main clause)**

This makes sense on its own.

> **because his leg *hurt* (subordinate clause)**

This is an adverbial clause saying why he limped.

Now look at the next sentence. It has *two* subordinate clauses. Again, the verbs are in italics.

> **Rose, who *was* a greedy girl, *ate* five cakes when she *came* home from school.**

> **Rose *ate* five cakes (main clause)**

> **who *was* a greedy girl (subordinate clause)**

This is an adjectival clause describing *Rose*.

> **when she *came* home from school (subordinate clause)**

Notice that each clause contains a verb.

This is an adverbial clause modifying *ate*.

Subordinate clauses can come at the *beginning* or *end* of a sentence. The subordinate clauses below are in italics.

> **She took her dog with her *wherever she went*.**

> ***Wherever she went* she took her dog with her.**

You can have a subordinate clause at the beginning, the main clause in the middle and the other subordinate clause at the end.

> ***When Tom got up* he put on his brown suit, *which was very smart*.**

This is the main clause.

26

Direct and reported speech

When you are writing sentences that contain somebody's speech you have to think carefully whether it is *direct* or *reported (indirect)* speech.

Direct speech

If you are writing down the exact words that someone is saying, or has said, it is called *direct* speech. The words actually spoken are put inside inverted commas (sometimes called quotation marks).

"I *am feeling* ill, Mum," said Fred.

I am feeling ill.

"What *have* you *been eating*?" she asked.

Reported (indirect) speech

You can, however, report what someone said in your own words. This is called *reported* or *indirect* speech. In this case you do not need inverted commas.

Fred told his Mum *he was feeling* ill.

She asked him what *he had been eating*.

Some of the verbs in the above sentences are in italics. These are the verbs included in the speech. If you look at the verbs in the *reported* speech you will notice that they are in the past tense. This is because you are writing down what happened in the past. The action is now over.

Direct speech

Remember the *tense* of each verb in reported speech goes back *one stage in time*.

Reported speech

"I *am* happy." – (He said) he *was* happy.
"I *saw* it." – (He said) he *had seen* it.

The future changes like this:

"I *shall* do it." – (He said) he *would* do it.

Could you be a reporter?

Can you re-write Lady Bloggs' speech in your own words?

"Welcome everyone! It is wonderful to see so many of you here today supporting our Charity Bazaar. I do hope you will all give generously to this worthy cause. Last year we made two thousand pounds at the same event and I hope we may make *even* more this year. There are many stalls and attractions which I am sure you will find entertaining . . ."

Word order in sentences

The meaning of a sentence depends not only on the words you use but also the order in which they appear. Most of the time you put words in the right order without even having to think about it, but there are one or two tricky instances when it is easy to make mistakes.

Misplaced words

When you use common adverbs* you need to think quite carefully about where you place them. They should be immediately before the words they modify. The word *just* is a good example of one of these adverbs. Notice the difference in meaning between the sentences below.

I *just* told my mother what I had seen.	(I recently told my mother.)
I told *just* my mother what I had seen.	(I told only my mother.)
I told my mother *just* what I had seen.	(I told my mother exactly what I had seen.)
I told my mother what I had *just* seen.	(I told my mother what I had recently seen.)

Misplaced phrases

Sometimes whole phrases can get into the wrong position in a sentence. This can make the meaning unclear or ridiculous.

The teacher kept the child who misbehaved *in the corner*.

Did the child misbehave in the corner?

Or was the child kept in the corner because he misbehaved?

Try to put phrases as close as possible to the word or words they relate to most closely. This is particularly important when you are dealing with phrases that have verbs ending in "-ing" or "-ed".

We saw some poppies walking *round the field*.

Put this phrase at the beginning of the sentence. It describes "we", not the "poppies".

28

*See pages 16-17.

Misplaced clauses

Clauses which describe someone or something should be placed as near as possible to the person or thing they describe.

This word order makes it sound as though the cliffs were screeching.

I heard the seagulls near the cliffs *that were screeching*.

This clause needs to go nearer to the seagulls.

Split infinitives

An infinitive is the part of the verb that has "to" in front of it.

**to hop
to skip
to jump**

These are all infinitives.

It is nearly always a mistake to split "to" from the verb if you are using an infinitive.

The detective decided *to* slowly and carefully *study* the clues. X

"To" and "study" should be next to each other.

The detective decided *to study* the clues slowly and carefully. ✓

Split verb and subject

The subject of a sentence should not be too far away from the verb because the meaning of the sentence can then become hard to follow.

Albert, after upsetting the basket and cracking all the eggs, *hid* in the cupboard. X

"Albert" needs to be nearer "hid".

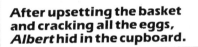

After upsetting the basket and cracking all the eggs, *Albert* hid in the cupboard. ✓

Wrong order

Can you spot the mistakes in the sentences below?:

1. I saw a frog fishing by the river.
2. The policeman arrested the man who was drunk quickly.
3. I saw the dog with its owner which was barking.
4. Ben, after eating ten chocolate bars, was sick.
5. She decided to gradually acquire a suntan.

Making the subject and verb agree

The subject of a sentence is who or what the sentence is about. It is in charge of or "governs" the verb. A singular subject means that the verb must be singular; a plural subject means that the verb must be plural.

Singular subject

This *cake is* stale.

Singular verb

These *cakes are* stale.

Plural subject

Plural verb

This is called making the subject and verb agree.

A group of words as a subject

If the subject is a group of words, rather than just one word, it is easy to make a mistake. Here the phrase "of potatoes" describing the subject can be mistaken for the subject itself.

A sack of potatoes *were* lying in the shed. X

Subject phrase

Decide which word is the subject by asking yourself *who* or *what* performed the action. Then think whether it is singular or plural and make the verb agree with it.

Singular subject

A *sack* of potatoes *was* lying in the shed. ✓

Singular verb

More than one verb

Sometimes one subject governs more than one verb. Make sure that all the verbs governed by a subject agree with it.

This *kind* of motorbike *looks* impressive but actually *do* not go very fast. X

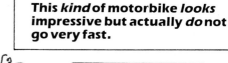

This should be *does* because the subject is "kind".

Don't make mistakes like this.

Whenever you have difficulty deciding whether a verb should be singular or plural, find the subject and ask yourself whether it is singular or plural.

More common mistakes

1. Words like anyone, everyone, someone, no one, each (indefinite pronouns), are singular and should take a *singular* verb.

Everyone *is* going on a picnic today.

Singular verb

The words many, both, few and several always take a *plural* verb.

Several of us *are* going swimming.

Plural verb

2. When you use "neither ... nor" in a sentence it can be difficult to decide what to do with the verbs.

If both the subjects are singular use a singular verb.

Neither the dog nor the cat *likes* the way Tom plays his violin.

If one or both subjects are plural, the verb is plural.

Neither Ben nor his brothers *like* having a bath.

3. Collective nouns (words which describe groups of persons or things) usually take a *singular* verb.

Class 4B
Ted's family
This football team
Tony's gang
} **is brilliant.**

4. When a sentence has more than one subject joined by "and" the verb should be *plural*.

Here *come* Annie and her sister. ✓

There are two subjects so the verb is plural.

Here *comes* Annie and her sister. ✗

Spot the mistakes

Can you spot the wrong agreement in these sentences?

1. This dog are vicious.
2. These tomatoes is ripe.
3. A box of chocolates are sitting on the table.
4. Rod's gang are very large.
5. James and Lucy is going away today.
6. Neither Sid nor his friends is coming to my party.
7. Here comes the bride and groom.
8. Class 2B are very noisy.
9. Here are two apples: both is ripe.
10. A few of us *is* here.

Words easily confused

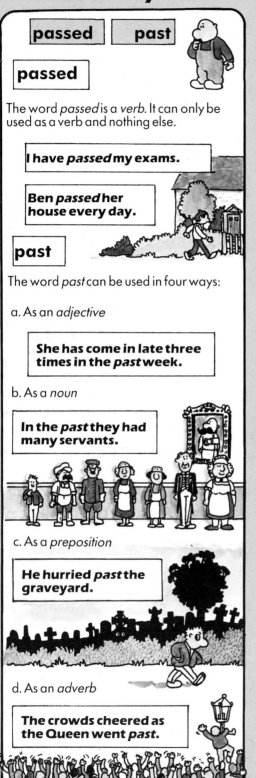

passed   past

passed

The word *passed* is a *verb*. It can only be used as a verb and nothing else.

> I have *passed* my exams.

> Ben *passed* her house every day.

past

The word *past* can be used in four ways:

a. As an *adjective*

> She has come in late three times in the *past* week.

b. As a *noun*

> In the *past* they had many servants.

c. As a *preposition*

> He hurried *past* the graveyard.

d. As an *adverb*

> The crowds cheered as the Queen went *past*.

off   of

These two words mean totally different things.

off

> "Get *off* my land!" shouted the farmer.

> She rubbed the dust *off* her shoes.

of

This sounds like *ov* when you say it because of the one "f".

> She climbed out *of* bed sleepily.

> Three *of* them wore hats.

Try not to confuse *of* with the word *have*.

Look at the sentence below:

> I *should have* gone with them.

Sometimes the words in italics are shortened to *should've*. This often sounds like *should of*.

Watch out for the words below:

> could've (could have)
> would've (would have)
> might've (might have)
> must've (must have)
> may've (may have)

Never say or write *could of*, etc.

we're | were

we're

We're is a shortened form (contraction) of the pronoun *we* and the verb *are*.

> **We're going away tomorrow.**
> **We are going away tomorrow.**

were

This is part of the verb "to be". It is part of the past tense of the verb.

> **They *were* very
> happy to be going
> away.**

Helpful hint: If you cannot remember which of these words to use, think: "Can I replace it with two words?" If you *can*, you use the shortened form "we're". It's the same with "who's".

---

who's | whose

who's

This is the shortened form (contraction) of the pronoun *who*[1] and either the verb *is* or the verb *has*.

> **Who's (who is) coming
> to the party?
> Who's (who has) been
> drinking my wine?**

whose

This word can be two parts of speech:

a. A *relative pronoun*[2] which shows ownership on behalf of the noun it relates to.

> **This is the man *whose* dog bit me.**

"Whose" refers back to the noun "man".

b. A *possessive adjective*[3] which refers to the noun it is next to.

> ***Whose* dog is this?**

---

affect | effect

affect

The word *affect* is a verb which means "to cause a change in something".

> **Sue changed her job because it
> *affected* her health.**

effect

This is a noun which means "result" or "consequence".

> **The change in job had a good
> *effect* and she was no longer
> ill.**

but

The word *effect* is sometimes used as a verb which means "to bring something into being".

> **The doctor hoped he
> could *effect* a cure for the
> disease.**

33

---

[1]See pages 6-7.   [2]See page 7.   [3]See pages 8-9.

Words often misused

teach   learn

teach

A teacher "teaches" someone how to do something. He gives out knowledge.

Jim is *teaching* me how to play the guitar.

learn

This word means "to take in" knowledge.

I *learned* to play the guitar very quickly with Jim as a teacher.

 You *cannot* "learn" someone how to do something.

lend   borrow

lend

This word means "to hand out" for a certain period of time.

"I will *lend* you a ruler," said Ben.

borrow

This word means "to take from" for a certain period of time.

She *borrowed* Ben's ruler for a few minutes.

You lend *to* someone and borrow *from* someone.

saw   seen

saw

This word is a verb. It makes sense on its own.

I *saw* a film last night.

seen

This word is only *part* of a verb. It needs an auxiliary verb* with it to help to make sense.

I *have seen* three films this week.

You cannot write:

I *seen* three films this week. ✗

did   done

did

The word *did* is a complete verb which makes sense on its own.

Dad *did* the washing.

done

The word *done* is only part of a verb. It needs an auxiliary verb* to make sense.

Dad *has done* the washing.

not

Dad *done* the washing. ✗

 "done" needs a *helping* verb with it.

*See page 12.

as like

as

This word always needs a verb to follow it.

> **She did it _as_ I _told_ her to.**

like

This word is followed by a noun or pronoun only.

> **She looks _like_ him.**

> **That man is driving _like_ a madman.**

Do not write:

> **She did it _like_ I told her to.** ✗

who which

These words are relative pronouns.*
This means they take the place of a noun and join two phrases or clauses.
Who is always used to refer to people.
Which is always used to refer to animals or things.

who

Look at these two sentences:

> **I have two brothers.
> My brothers are fat.**

You can join these sentences together with a relative pronoun.

> **I have two brothers _who_ are fat.**

"Who" takes the place of the noun "brothers".

which

The same applies to the word _which_.

> **She has three cats.
> The cats are Siamese.**

> **She has three cats _which_ are Siamese.**

"Which" takes the place of the noun "cats".

can may might

can

This word means "capable of doing".

> **I _can_ go out now.**

> **I _can_ speak French well.**

may

This word is used in two ways:

1. To ask permission to do something.

> **_May_ I go out now?**

Although nowadays people often say or write:

> **"_Can_ we have lunch now?"** ✗

You _should_ say:

> **"_May_ we have lunch now?"** ✓

2. You also use the word _may_ when there is a fair possibility that something will happen.

> **The princess _may_ visit this town tomorrow.**

This means it is quite possible.

might

This is used when there is less possibility of something happening.

> **The princess _might_ visit this town tomorrow.**

This means there is a possibility but that it is not very likely.

*See page 7.

Other problems

Here are some common mistakes which seem to crop up frequently in written and spoken English.

Slang

Everyone talks in "slang" sometimes. There are many words and phrases used in everyday speech and writing which are called slang. They are often funny expressions but should not be used in formal speech or writing.

Spot the slang

The sentences below are written in slang. Can you re-write them in formal English?

1. I'm fed up with this job, I'm going to pack it in.
2. John is keen on a bird up the road.
3. We thought Jane was stuck up but she was just feeling out of sorts.
4. Tim's father is in the nick because someone grassed on him.
5. Mum has flipped her lid because Bill has pushed off without telling her.
6. I'm so hard up I can't get to the movies.
7. Dad went round the bend when I told him to get lost.
8. She slogs her guts out working for a boss who's a pain in the neck.

Double negatives

A *negative* is a word which gives the meaning of "no" or "not". If you put *two* negatives in one sentence they will cancel each other out and you will lose the negative meaning altogether.

Look at this sentence:

X **I *don't* want *nothing*.**

There are *two* negatives here.

You should write:

I *don't* want *anything*. ✓

or

I want *nothing*. ✓

He's *not* seen *neither* of them. X

He's *not* seen either of them. ✓

or

He's seen *neither* of them. ✓

Jumping tenses

When you write a sentence or a passage you should always be consistent about the tense of the verb. If you start to write about something in the past, you must keep to the past all the way through. If you start to write in the present then you must continue in the present.

Look at the sentences below:

They walked through the forest and breathed in the scent of pine. It *is* cool and fresh and they *feel* as if they could stay forever.

What should the words in italics really be?

All the verbs are in the past tense except for *is* and *feel*. The tenses of these verbs have jumped to the present. This makes the passage rather confusing to the reader.

Odds and ends

hardly	**scarcely**

When these words mean "no sooner than" they are always followed closely by *when* or *before*, not the word *than*.

> He had scarcely left the house *when* the telephone rang.

> She had hardly eaten a mouthful *before* she felt sick.

No "than" here.

them	**those**

Sometimes people use the word *them* as an adjective instead of *those*.

Them is the object form of the pronoun *they*. It can *never* be used as an adjective.

Those can be used as a demonstrative adjective* or as a pronoun. Here it is an adjective.

> Give it to **them**.

> **Those** flowers are pretty.

Do *not* write or say:

> Pass me *them* books. ✗

It should be:

> Pass me *those* books. ✓

between

The word *between* is always followed by *and* not *or*.

> She had a choice between a white dress *and* a black one. ✓

not

> She had a choice between a white dress *or* a black one. ✗

to try *to*	**to try *and***

You normally use the word *to* after the verb to try. It is a common mistake to put the word *and*.

✓ > I am going to try *to* save money this year.

✗ > I am going to try *and* save money this year.

literally

This word means "exactly to the letter" or "in actual fact". You *cannot* write:

> Celia was *literally* rooted to the spot. ✗

This is possible.

You can write: ✓ > Celia literally fainted with shock.

unique

This word means the only one of its kind. You cannot say something is *quite* unique or *very* unique, it is either unique or not unique.

✓ | This precious vase is *unique*. | | This precious vase is *quite* unique. | ✗

*See pages 8-9.

Tips on writing good English

Good writing should be clear, simple and concise. This does not mean that the sentences you write should be abrupt and full of short, uncomplicated words. It is important to use a variety of words and ways of expressing things. But it is also important to make sure that each word you use contributes something to the meaning of the sentence.

Planning

First of all it will help if you spend some time planning what you are going to write before you start writing. List all the points or ideas that you want to include and think carefully about how you are going to link or contrast them. Read through what you have planned, to see if you have forgotten anything.

Paragraphs

The way you arrange words on a page and the amount of space you leave around them also helps your reader to understand the exact meaning of your words.

Divide your writing into paragraphs to help your reader. A paragraph is a set of sentences. There is no rule about how many sentences there should be in a paragraph; just use as many as makes a digestible piece of reading. But do try to end one paragraph and begin another at a point where it is logical to have a slight break.

The first line of a paragraph is set inwards from the margin (indented) to make it easier to see where each paragraph begins.

You usually start a new paragraph when introducing into the story:

1. A person.

2. A new place.

3. A change of time.

4. A change of idea.

If you are writing down a conversation you always start a new paragraph every time one person stops speaking and another person starts. This makes it easier for the reader to tell who is speaking which words.

Take special care with the opening and closing paragraphs of what you write. The opening paragraph will decide whether you capture your reader's interest; the closing paragraph will determine the impression he is left with.

Reading through

As you read through, you may also spot some spelling mistakes or missing punctuation.

When you have finished writing, read through what you have written. Think about your reader or readers. Try to put yourself in their position and see whether you can understand what you have written. Ask yourself whether it will hold their interest and whether it states accurately what you want to tell them.

Things to avoid

1. *Repetition.* Your writing can become very boring for your reader if you keep repeating the same words or phrases unnecessarily.

The same word is used too many times.

> **We visited a most *mysterious* house. There was a *mysterious* secret passage which led out to a walled garden. All the plants in the garden were white or grey which gave the place a very *mysterious* atmosphere.**

2. *Overworked words.* Certain words tend to be used too much, so that their meaning becomes vague and woolly. They can be acceptable when used in just the right place, but it is better to think of a more precise alternative to replace them.

> nice lovely fantastic terrific great incredible horrible funny dreadful fine good get

There are lots of other overworked words.

3. *Clichés.* These are phrases that have been used over and over again until all their freshness and originality has disappeared. Try to think of your own way of expressing something instead of resorting to stock phrases.

> ***In this day and age* I think it is important for *each and every one of us, right across the board,* to *stand up and be counted.***

4. *Ambiguity.* This is when there is more than one meaning to a sentence and there is no way of telling which one the writer intended. This often happens when a word or phrase is put in the wrong position.

> **The fire was put out before any damage could be done by the fire brigade.**

It can also happen when you use pronouns without making it quite clear to whom they refer.

> **If the baby does not eat its supper, throw it away.**

5. *Tautology.* This is the use of an extra word or phrase which pointlessly repeats an idea in the sentence.

> **The annual party at Castle Crum is held every year.**

"Annual" is the same as "every year".

You could say either:

> **There is an annual party at Castle Crum.**

or

> **The party at Castle Crum is held every year.**

6. *Verbosity.* Using too many words where plain, straightforward language would be more effective, will make what you write sound pompous and unnatural. Try not to use long words where short ones are just as effective, or more words than are necessary to express your meaning.

> **At this moment in time I am of the opinion that it is of the utmost importance to labour diligently at whatsoever matter may fall to your lot.**

> **I now think that it is very important to work hard at whatever you do.**

39

Test yourself

How many pronouns?

Can you spot all the pronouns in these sentences?

> 1. I don't know which of them is going to help with this
> 2. She collected the parcel herself.
> 3. "To whom does that belong?" he asked angrily.
> 4. "These are ready, but those aren't," I said.
> 5. "Who do you think will be coming tonight?" she asked.
> 6. He has a car which he will lend us.

Don't forget! There are different *kinds* of pronouns. See page 7.

Which kind of noun?

In the eight sentences below there are 31 nouns. Can you find them all and decide which kind they are? (common, proper, collective or abstract?)

> 1. Everyone lived in fear of Charlie and his gang of thugs.
> 2. A flock of sheep ambled across the road, causing a huge traffic-jam.
> 3. Mary ran down the High Street to catch the bus, which was stopping outside the Odeon Cinema.
> 4. Claude was a Frenchman who came from Paris.
> 5. The jury took a long time to decide whether or not the prisoner had told the truth.
> 6. A fleet of ships sailed out of the harbour at great speed.
> 7. The farmer asked the vet to have a look at his herd of cows.
> 8. The crocodile gobbled up a shoal of fish.

See page 5 if you are stuck.

Comparing things

Can you fill in the missing words or letters below?

> 1. Jane is pretty but Sarah is even prett. . . .
> 2. Of the three boys, James is the fat. . . . .
> 3. My house is large, Tom's is larg . . ., but Dan's house is the larg . . . .
> 4. John's behaviour is bad, but Tim's is . . . . .
> 5. The old lady had only a little money, her friend had even . . . . . , but the man round the corner had the . . . . . .

Phrase or clause?

In the sentences below, the words in italics form either a phrase or a clause. Can you sort out which is which?

Remember, a phrase does not have a verb in it.

1. The women *in the audience* began to faint.
2. They travelled wearily *across the desert*.
3. *When she was young* Doris was very attractive.
4. Tom ran *along the road, round the corner* and *into the house*.
5. James bought a new cassette *when he went shopping*.
6. The man *in the dark glasses* looked very mysterious.
7. Kim, *who is an eccentric person*, collects extremely unusual teapots.
8. Peter was a bully *whom everybody feared*.
9. Sue kept a goat *in her front garden*.

Spot the mistakes

There are 13 mistakes in the sentences below. Can you find them all?

1. "Who's book is this?" she asked.
2. "Whose coming to the party?" asked Sarah.
3. "I don't know whether these pills will have any affect," said the doctor.
4. She fell of her bicycle because off the hole in the road.
5. "You should of known better," said the teacher.
6. "Mum, will you learn me how to cook that dish?" she asked.
7. "Can I lend your car, Jim?" asked Jo.
8. "I seen four burglars come out of that house," she told the police.
9. Tom did the job like I told him to.
10. Jane done four hours' work last night.
11. She has four sisters which are all younger than her.
12. Henrietta has five white mice who are all female.

Participles quiz

Verb, adjective or noun? Can you work out how the participles have been used in the sentences below? (The participles are in italics.)

1. Alfie has *learnt* to walk already.
2. The acrobats performed an amazing *balancing* act.
3. The neighbours have *moved* out this week.
4. "That's seven years' bad luck," she said as she looked at the *broken* mirror.
5. *The fighting* in the playground worried the headmaster.
6. The *screaming* girls chased the filmstar down the road.
7. The baby next door is *teething*.
8. *The singing* in the chapel was a delight to her ears.

Missing prepositions

Can you think of suitable prepositions to fill the gaps below?

Charlie got . . . . early. He put . . . . his clothes and went . . . . the stairs . . . . the kitchen. He sat . . . . the table . . . . the window and looked . . . . the garden and saw his father sitting . . . . a tree. When he had finished eating he went . . . . the door, ... of the house and . . . . the garden to join his father. He sat . . . . him on the ground and looked seriously . . . . his eyes. "Can you lend me some money, Dad?" he asked.

What can you find?

There are 15 verbs, 27 adjectives and 10 adverbs in this story. Can you find them all?

In the middle of a dark, forbidding forest lived a strange, old man. His home was a rickety little shack which had two cracked windows and a creaking door.

The man lived quite alone except for the company of a thin, bedraggled cat, and a large, lazy dog.

Each day he wandered off among the tall pine-trees and whistled softly to himself. He only returned to his humble home late in the evening when the sun had gone down.

Then he would sit quietly by the flickering fire and warm his gnarled hands; or he would talk gently to the animals as he tossed them scraps of his meagre supper.

Despite his simple existence, the old man was content. He troubled no one, and no one troubled him.

Answers

Spot the noun (page 4)

Pick out the nouns

box
David
dog
cup
bottle

How many nouns?

18 nouns.	Cynthia	rabbit	bicycle
	dress	budgerigar	man
Boris	Tom	Mary	bed
cat	dog	car	table
road	hamster	favour	chair

Find the pronouns (page 7)

1. She, them.
2. We, him, he.
3. I, this, yours, she.
4. You, her, she, us.
5. It, yours, it, mine.
6. They, me, them.

Spot the verb (page 12)

1. cleaned
2. is barking
3. has made
4. will be watching
5. has crashed
6. is tossing

Fill in the missing verb (page 12)

1. are
2. has
3. will
4. shall
5. will
6. is, *or* was
7. were, *or* are will be, have been.

Change around (page 13)

1. A huge, black spider *was eaten* by the cat.
2. The silver *is cleaned* by Doris every fortnight.
3. The lawn was *mowed* by Mum early this morning.
4. The money *was hidden* under the bed by the burglars.
5. The rubbish *was thrown* into the dustbin by Jo.
6. The horse *was brushed* by the groom.
7. The plants *are watered* by the gardener.
8. A taxi *was ordered* by him to take her home.

What is missing? (page 21)

1. because, as, since *or* while
2. but
3. whether, or
4. and, as well as.

Which pair? (page 21)

1. whether . . . or
2. not only . . . but also
3. either . . . or
4. neither . . . nor
5. both . . . and

Could you be a reporter? (page 27)

Possible answer: (Words in italics show change of tense.)

Lady Bloggs *welcomed* everyone. She said that it *was* wonderful to see so many people there supporting their Charity Bazaar and *hoped* they *would* all give generously to the worthy cause. She went on to say that last year they *had made* two thousand pounds at the same event and *hoped* that they *might* make even more this year. There *were* many stalls and attractions which she *was* sure they *would* find entertaining.

Wrong order (page 29)

1. Fishing by the river, I saw a frog.
2. The policeman quickly arrested the man who was drunk.
3. I saw the dog which was barking, with its owner.
4. Ben was sick after eating ten chocolate bars.
5. She decided to acquire a suntan gradually.

Spot the mistakes (page 31)

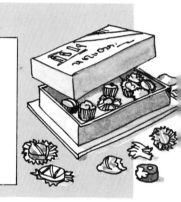

1. This dog *is* vicious.
2. These tomatoes *are* ripe.
3. A box of chocolates *is* sitting on the table.
4. Rod's gang *is* very large.
5. James and Lucy *are* going away tomorrow.
6. Neither Sid nor his friends *are* coming to my party.
7. Here *come* the bride and groom.
8. Class 2B *is* very noisy.
9. Here are two apples: both *are* ripe.
10. A few of us *are* here.

How many pronouns? (page 40)

19 pronouns.
1. I, which, them, this.
2. She, herself.
3. Whom, that, he
4. These, those, I.
5. Who, you, she.
6. He, which, he, us.

Which kind of noun? (page 40)

1. *Common:* thugs, sheep, road, traffic-jam, bus, prisoner ships, harbour, farmer, vet, look, cows, crocodile, fish.
2. *Proper:* Charlie, Mary, High Street, Odeon Cinema, Claude, Frenchman, Paris.
3. *Collective:* gang, flock, jury, fleet, herd, shoal.
4. *Abstract:* fear, truth, speed, time.

Comparing things (page 40)

1. Jane is pretty but Sarah is even prett*er*.
2. Of the three boys, James is the fatt*est*.
3. My house is large, Tom's is larg*er*, but Dan's house is the larg*est*.
4. John's behaviour is bad, but Tim's is *worse*.
5. The old lady had only a little money, her friend had even *less*, but the man round the corner had the *least*.

Phrase or clause (page 41)

1. phrase
2. phrase
3. clause
4. 3 phrases
5. clause
6. phrase
7. clause
8. clause
9. phrase

Spot the mistakes (page 41)

1. *Whose* book is this? she asked.
2. "*Who's* coming to the party?" asked Sarah.
3. "I don't know whether these pills will have any *effect*," said the doctor.
4. She fell *off* her bicycle because *of* the hole in the road.
5. "You should'*ve* (have) known better," said the teacher.
6. "Mum, will you *teach* me how to cook that dish?" she asked.
7. "Can I *borrow* your car, Jim?" asked Jo.
8. "I *saw* four burglars come out of that house," she told the police.
9. Tom did the job *as* I told him to.
10. Jane *did* four hours' work last night.
11. She has four sisters *who* are all younger than her.
12. Henrietta has five white mice *which* are all female.

Participles quiz (page 42)

1. verb
2. adjective
3. verb
4. adjective
5. noun (gerund)
6. adjective
7. verb
8. noun (gerund)

Missing prepositions (page 42)

up, on, down, into (to), at, by (near or beside), across (into), under, through, out, into, beside (near), into

What can you find (page 42)

Verbs — 14, lived (× 2), was, had, wandered, whistled, returned, had gone would sit, warm, would talk, tossed, was, troubled (×2).

Adjectives — 27, dark, forbidding, strange, old (× 2), rickety, little, two, cracked, creaking, thin, bedraggled, large, lazy, each, tall, humble, flickering, gnarled, meagre, simple, content, his (× 5).

Adverbs — 10, quite, alone, off, softly, only, late, down, then, quietly, gently.

Literary terms – More tips on writing English

If you want to write in an interesting and lively way you may want to include some of the following:-

Similes

A simile compares two things, bringing out a point of "likeness" between the two things.

> **She was shaking like a leaf.**

The most common words which introduce a simile are:

> as, like, as if, as though, as . . . as.

Metaphors

A metaphor is like a simile except that it compares two things by saying that one thing *is* something else. It does not use the word "like" or "as".

> **That man is an ass.**

Alliteration

This is the repeating of a particular letter or sound (usually consonants at the beginning of words) to produce an interesting effect.

> **She sat sipping soda in the sizzling sun.**

Onomatopoeia

This is the use of words which imitate or suggest the sound of what they describe.

> **The ducks *quacked* and *splashed* in the water.**

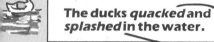

> If you say these words aloud you can *hear* how similar they are to the noise they describe.

This use of words can intensify the meaning of what you write. It is often used in poetry.

Synonym

This is a word that has almost the same meaning as another word. Here are some

> small – tiny, little, minute

If you need to describe the same thing twice but want to avoid repetition you should use a synonym. It is a "stand-in" for the word it replaces.

> **Cynthia had *large* feet. In fact her feet were so *immense* she had to have *huge* shoes especially made for her.**

> If you use a synonym or an antonym it must be the same part of speech as the word it replaces.

Antonym

This is a word which has a meaning opposite to another word.

> slow – fast   work – relax

You may want to use an antonym to add a contrast in feeling or description.

> **All day Jane behaved like an *angel*, but her brother Sam was more like a *devil*.**

46

Index/glossary

abstract noun, 5 Noun which describes things that cannot actually be seen, heard, smelt or tasted: e.g. love, hate.

active voice, 13 The "voice" of the verb which shows that the subject of the sentence is performing the action.

adjectival clause, 25, 26 Clause which acts as an adjective and therefore describes a noun or pronoun.

adjectival phrase, 15, 24 Phrase which acts as an adjective and therefore describes a noun or pronoun.

adjective, 3, 8, 9, 14, 15, 16, 17, 23, 32, 37 Describing word which gives a fuller meaning to a noun: e.g. *pretty* girl.

adverb, 3, 16, 17, 18, 23, 32 Word which "modifies" or tells you more information about a verb, adjective or other adverb. Usually answers the questions How? When? Where? or Why? in connection with the verb.

adverbial clause, 25, 26 Clause which does the work of an adverb.

adverbial phrase, 16, 23, 24 Phrase which does the work of an adverb.

adverb of degree, 16, 17 Adverb which can also modify adjectives and other adverbs. Always answers the question How much? e.g. She worked *very* hard.

alliteration, 46 The repeating of a particular letter or sound at the beginning of words to produce an interesting effect.

ambiguity, 39 When a sentence or passage has more than one meaning and the reader has no way of telling which one the writer intended.

antonym, 46 Word which has the opposite meaning to another word: e.g. hot-cold.

auxiliary verb, 12, 34, 35 A "helping" verb. Some verbs are made up of more than one word: e.g. he *is whistling*, they *are eating*. The verbs "to be" and "to have" are auxiliary verbs.

clause, 16, 20, 21, 26, 29 Group of words containing a subject and a verb. There are two kinds: (1) main clause; (2) subordinate clause. The main clause makes complete sense on its own, but a subordinate clause is dependent on the main clause for its sense: e.g. He ate a loaf of bread (main clause), because he was hungry (subordinate clause).

cliché, 39 Phrase which has been used over and over again until its freshness and originality have disappeared.

collective noun, 5, 31 Noun which describes a group or collection of people or things: e.g. team, pack, swarm.

command, 22 A sentence which gives an order or request. (The subject is usually understood and not mentioned.)

common adverb, 17, 28 Adverb used for emphasis. Must be placed near the word it modifies to avoid confusion.

common noun, 5 Word used as the name of a person, thing or place: e.g. dog, man.

comparative adjective, 9 Adjective used to *compare* two people or things. Usually ends in -er.

complex sentence, 26 A sentence which is made up of a main clause with one or more subordinate clauses. Each clause always contains a subject and verb: e.g. The teacher *helped* the child (main clause) who *did* not understand (subordinate clause).

compound sentence, 23 A sentence made up of two or more simple sentences joined by a conjunction or separated by a comma, semi-colon or colon.

conjunction, 3, 20, 21, 23, 26 Word used to connect clauses or sentences; or to connect words within a clause.

continuous tense, 11, 14 The tense of the verb which shows that the action is going on for some time.

contraction, 33 Shortened form of two words, using an apostrophe: e.g. we are — we're.

co-ordinating conjunction, 21 Conjunction used to join two sentences of equal importance: e.g. and, but, or, yet.

demonstrative adjective, 8 Adjective which "points out" something: e.g. *this* child.

demonstrative pronoun, 7 Type of pronoun which points out a person or thing specifically: e.g. this, that, these, those.

direct speech, 27 The exact words that someone speaks: e.g. "How are you?"

double negative, 36 This is when two negatives are used together, with the effect of cancelling each other out. The negative meaning is then lost.

exclamation, 3, 22 Word or sentences used to express strong feeling or emotion.

gender, 5 The classification of words according to whether they are masculine, feminine or neuter.

gerund, 15 A participle used as a noun. It acts like any other noun, therefore it can be described by an adjective. It can be the subject or object of the sentence.

indefinite pronoun, 7 Pronoun which refers to people or things generally, rather than specifically: e.g. any, each, several.

indirect speech, 27 — See "reported speech".

infinitive, 11 The *name* of the verb. It usually has "to" in front of it, but you can use it without.

interjection, 3 Word used to express exclamation: e.g. Oh!

interrogative adjective, 8 Adjective which "asks" something about the noun.

interrogative pronoun, 7 A pronoun which helps to ask a question or "interrogate": e.g. who? whose? which?

intransitive verb, 10 Verb which does not carry the action to an object.

inverted commas, 27 Punctuation marks used to show the exact words that someone has spoken.

main clause, 21, 25, 26 See "clause".

metaphor, 46 This is a phrase or sentence which compares two things by saying that something *is* something else: e.g. Her face was a picture.

negative, 36 A word which gives the meaning of "no" or "not".

noun, 3, 4, 5, 6, 8, 9, 15, 16, 18, 24, 25, 31, 32, 35 See "common noun".

noun clause, 25, 26 Clause which can take the place of a noun. It can be the subject or object of the verb.

noun phrase, 24 Phrase which acts as a noun.

object, 6, 10, 19, 25 This tells you "what" or "whom" the verb in a sentence affects.

onomatopoeia, 46 Use of words which imitate or suggest the sound of what they describe.

paragraph, 38 Passage or section of writing marked off by indenting the first line.

participle, 14, 15, 28 Part of a verb. Can be past or present. (1) Present participle is part of verb that usually ends in -*ing*: e.g. making, laughing, working; (2) Past participle is the part of the verb which follows "have" or "has" in the past tense.

passive voice, 13 This is the "voice" of the verb which shows that the subject is having the action done to it.

personal pronoun, 7 The kind of pronoun used most often. Usually stands instead of someone speaking, being spoken to, or spoken of: e.g. "I was waiting for *you* with *him*."

phrase, 16, 20, 23, 24, 28, 30 Small group of words without a verb, which is not a complete sentence.

plural, 4, 6, 30, 31 This means more than one person or thing: e.g. book*s*.

possessive adjective, 8, 15, 33 Adjective which shows ownership: e.g. *my* pen.

predicate, 22, 23 A sentence can be divided into subject and predicate. The *predicate* is what is written or said about the subject. It always contains a verb: e.g. Flossie (subject) *baked a cake* (predicate).

preposition, 3, 7, 18, 19, 26, 32 Word used for showing what one person or thing has to do with another person or thing – usually where they are in relation to one another.

pronoun, 3, 6, 7, 8, 9, 12, 15, 16, 18, 19, 35, 37 Word which stands instead of a noun. There are many kinds of pronoun including *possessive, reflexive* and *personal* pronouns.

proper noun, 5 Noun which refers to a particular person or thing, rather than a general class of things: e.g. Paris, David.

question, 22 A sentence which asks for an answer: e.g. Is it raining?

quotation marks, 27 See "inverted commas".

reflexive pronoun, 7 Pronoun which *reflects* back to an earlier noun or pronoun: e.g. myself, yourself, himself.

relative pronoun, 7 A pronoun which helps to connect or relate one part of the sentence to another: e.g. who, that.

reported speech, 27 Speech which is "reported" back in your own words. It is not accompanied by inverted commas: e.g. She said that she was late.

sentence, 6, 7, 10, 13, 16, 17, 20, 22, 23, 24, 25, 26, 27, 28 A word or group of words which makes complete sense on its own.

sentence adverb, 17 Adverb which is inserted into a sentence to alter the meaning in some way: e.g. moreover, nevertheless, however.

simile, 46 A phrase which compares two things, bringing out a "point of likeness" between them: e.g. as white as snow.

simple sentence, 23 A sentence with only *one* subject and *one* predicate.

singular, 4, 6, 30, 31 This means one single person or thing: e.g. man, book.

slang, 36 General words and phrases that are in common use, but are not considered to be part of standard English.

split infinitives, 29 This is when an adverb or phrase comes between "to" and the rest of the verb: e.g. to completely *deny*, to badly *need*. They should be avoided.

statement, 22 A sentence which states a fact.

subject, 6, 10, 22, 23, 24, 25, 30, 31 The person or thing doing the action in a sentence.

subordinate clause, 21, 25, 26 See "clause".

subordinating conjunction, 21 A conjunction which introduces a subordinate clause and links it to the main clause: e.g. because, if, while.

superlative adjective, 9 Adjective used to indicate the highest degree of comparison. Refers to at least three people or things.

synonym, 46 A word which has almost the same meaning as another word.

tense, 11, 12, 14, 27, 36 The tense of a verb tells you the time at which the action takes place. There are three main tenses: past, present and future.

tautology, 39 The use of an extra word or phrase which pointlessly repeats an idea in the sentence.

transitive verb, 10 Verb which takes the action of the sentence from the subject to the object.

verb, 3, 10, 11, 12, 13, 14, 16, 22, 23, 24, 25, 27, 30, 31, 34 Word which shows some kind of action or being: e.g. run.

First published in 1983 by Usborne Publishing Ltd, Usborne House, 83-85 Saffron Hill, London EC1N 8RT, England.

© 1990, 1983 Usborne Publishing